THE EFFICIENT FAMILY OFFICE

WHY YOU SHOULD (AND CAN) BUILD YOUR OWN FINANCIAL DREAM TEAM LIKE THE WORLD'S WEALTHIEST FAMILIES

THE EFFICIENT FAMILY OFFICE

WHY YOU SHOULD (AND CAN) BUILD YOUR OWN FINANCIAL DREAM TEAM LIKE THE WORLD'S WEALTHIEST FAMILIES

MICHAEL MCDERMOTT

ethos
collective

Published by Igniting Souls
PO Box 43, Powell, OH 43065
IgnitingSouls.com

LCCN: 2024912317
Paperback ISBN: 978-1-63680-319-7
Hardcover ISBN: 978-1-63680-320-3
e-book ISBN: 978-1-63680-321-0

Available in paperback, hardcover, e-book, and audiobook.

Table of Contents

Tribute to the Kathmere Capital Team

As CEO, I feel privileged to lead this remarkable team, but our story is far greater than any individual's achievements. This book is a tribute to the collective efforts of Kathmere, written on behalf of every member who has contributed to our success.

Kathmere Capital stands as the driving force behind The Efficient Family Office process—an innovative approach that sets us apart in the world of wealth management. But our journey to this point has been anything but solitary. It's been a collaborative effort, with every team member lending their expertise to build the systems and processes that define us today.

I am profoundly grateful to each and every person on the Kathmere team who has played a role in enhancing the way we operate. Every single individual has left an indelible mark on our company's journey.

But our work is far from over. Every day, we strive to raise the bar, constantly refining our value proposition to provide our clients with a truly exceptional experience. At Kathmere, we believe in the power of continuous improvement, the depth of our company's capabilities, and the unique value we bring to our clients.

As you embark on this journey through the pages of our story, I believe you'll see Kathmere Capital as more than just a financial firm. I hope you'll feel the passion, dedication, and collective spirit that drives us forward every day.

Why Did I Write This Book?

Wayne Gretzky, the legendary ice hockey player, was famous for saying, "Good hockey players skate to where the puck has been; great players skate to where the puck will be." This philosophy encapsulates the essence of forward-thinking mindsets and strategic planning, not just in sports but also in life and business. In the financial world, this principle means that top advisory firms don't simply focus on the current landscape; they anticipate the shifts and trends shaping the future of the industry. While good advisors understand strategies for serving clients in today's environment, great advisory firms adapt and innovate to raise the bar on how to serve clients in ways that others aren't yet considering. I want this book to help you find an advisor who is skating to "where the puck will be."

Thanks to advancements in technology, leading firms are developing the ability to provide significantly more service and value for their clients, usually without changes to their fee structures. However, a segment of advisor-led clients remain unaware of these opportunities. Sadly, they still receive basic, narrow advice from their advisors. At Kathmere, we believe clients deserve more. They warrant personalized, comprehensive service that maximizes the value of their investment and, ultimately, optimizes their financial outcomes.

To help you see the potential in this type of next-level approach, I want to introduce you to the concept of the family office structure—the model employed by many of the nation's wealthiest families. Traditionally, these ultra-high-net-worth families have built teams of specialized investment, tax, and legal professionals to singularly focus on managing their financial affairs. Today, the power of technological advancements allows us to replicate many aspects of this structure in an effective and cost-effective manner.

Enter The Efficient Family Office—a service model designed to provide everything families with significant wealth need without the exorbitant costs associated with maintaining their own traditional family office. Kathmere Capital Management believes in offering our clients a consolidated, collaborative, and efficient approach to investment, estate planning, and tax strategy.

We like to say our Efficient Family Office model provides you with "Everything you need and nothing you don't." By harnessing the power of modern technology and adding our collective expertise, we empower clients to make informed decisions and maximize their financial potential. Together, we can skate where the puck is going to be and unlock the full potential of your financial future.

1

Who I Wrote This Book For

I n the mid-to-late 1990s, I embarked on a journey into the world of finance with a simple yet profound goal: to help clients achieve their financial aspirations. Unlike the seasoned professionals, I didn't have a vast team or decades of experience to rely on. It was just me, armed with a passion for making a meaningful impact on the lives of those I served. Over those early years, through a combination of grit and a bit of good luck, I managed to find enough people to put their trust in me to build my business, and my professional journey grew and expanded.

Looking back, I'm reminded of the vast array of clients we have been privileged to serve throughout the last several decades. From young professionals making their first mark on the world to seasoned investors managing substantial portfolios, we have served all types of people at all levels of wealth.

Some of my initial clients have remained close companions. I have enjoyed witnessing their aspirations transform into tangible realities and celebrating their milestones and triumphs along the way.

However, as time passed, our firm grew and matured. I brought on other professionals to help guide our diverse tapestry of clients, and with the growth of the firm, the average net worth of our clients increased as well. Today, we often find ourselves serving a different breed of clients compared to those I served in the 1990s—individuals who have accumulated significant wealth through their corporate careers, entrepreneurial endeavors, investments, and other ventures. This natural progression appears often in our industry. Nonetheless, these clients face a new set of challenges and opportunities. They demand specialized expertise and tailored solutions to address their complex financial needs.

Amidst this evolution, I never lost sight of those who stood by us from the beginning. Those clients who may not fit the conventional definition of "High Net Worth" remain an integral part of our story and still hold our deepest admiration. We still serve them with our highest efforts. We often find these meetings the most enjoyable. Perhaps because our history together is meaningful, and the progress we've made over time is often remarkable.

But as I sit to put pen to paper, I realize this book is not necessarily for all those early clients. It's not a dismissal but rather an acknowledgment of the growth they helped Kathmere to encounter and the opportunities that lie ahead. In that light, I want *The Efficient Family Office* to be a comprehensive guide crafted specifically for those who have achieved substantial wealth and now stand at the crossroads of complexity and opportunity.

The Efficient Family Office represents our unwavering commitment to client success and our relentless pursuit of innovation. As I unveil the unique strategies and solutions we've crafted to address the needs of our evolving clientele, I hope even our longest-tenured clients feel inspired by the spirit of "skating to where the puck will be" that drives us forward.

Not All Advisors Are Created Equal

In the realm of financial advising, a common misconception prevails. Too many people believe all advisors are cut from the same cloth. Yet, nothing could be further from the truth. Many advisors build fancy websites and articulate promises of exceptional care. They use fancy words about investment strategy and talk over the heads of clients who don't know what the industry jargon means. Very little of their online content can be used to decipher the advisor's competencies, and almost none of it has anything to do with your ultimate success. Sadly, discerning the differences among advisors can be a daunting task.

As someone deeply immersed in the financial world, I often find myself wishing I could give others a glimpse into the intricate knowledge and insight I've gleaned over the years. In fact, I believe if more high net-worth individuals understood the makings of a great wealth management professional, the well-intentioned, but often lower caliber, advisors would be weeded out, leaving only the truly exceptional to serve this level of client.

Athletes give us a great backdrop. Regardless of the type of athlete or the sport, we encounter a variety of skill levels. In youth sports, any standout player looks like the next Hall of Famer. At that novice level, it remains difficult to see their full potential. As the competitors mature, defining characteristics begin to emerge. By the time an athlete gets to the professional level, the difference between very good and legendary players, though indistinguishable at a lower level of competition, becomes abundantly clear.

Take golf, for example. I enjoy the sport, and it provides an analogy to which I can speak confidently. Every golf course has its celebrated low handicappers, otherwise known as their "scratch golfers." To the common golfer, these club members seem like legends, striping tee shots, making birdies, and rolling in putts like they belong on tour chasing down the Masters or US Open titles. However, when most of these "club champions" attempt to move up to their city or state amateur championship, their shortcomings begin to show. Suddenly, these top-course players look awfully normal and unremarkable. Only a select few top local players make the cut to forge ahead to the next level.

And with each move up the ladder, a few more fall. Club champions can't compete with city and state champions. City and state champions look like amateurs against college All-Americans. And amazingly, even these elite players have low odds of making the PGA Tour.

And on the PGA tour, of the multitude who attempt to play the circuit, only 125 to 150 get their PGA Tour card, less than 70 make the cut at the Masters or the Open, and only a few will ever be considered historically elite players like Tiger Woods or Jack Nicklaus. Suddenly, you realize your club's champion golfer sits at least ten levels away from the top tier.

So, how does this analogy tie back to the unfortunate reality that all advisors are not the same? Like athletes, only when the advisor is challenged at a higher level will the difference be seen. In simple financial situations, all advisors possessing a baseline level of competency may be qualified to assist. Most recommendations would be similar, delivering comparable results over time. However, move up one level in complexity, and some differences may become apparent. Skills, expertise, and team depth suddenly play a potentially greater role in creating the desired results. Move up again to an even more complex and intricate situation demanding a significantly higher level of planning needs, and the differences could make or break someone's financial situation. As we will touch on later in more detail, one reality with financial advice is that bad advice doesn't show itself as such immediately. In contrast with the dynamics of competitive golf, where scores quickly and decisively reveal that the pro-looking club golfer can't compete with PGA Tour pros, with financial advice, inferior advice comes with no such leaderboard to easily distinguish the truly excellent from the so-so.

You'll find many advisors who handle smaller accounts with excellence and possess a tremendous understanding of the basics. To the average client, these advisors seem to be at the top of their game. Unfortunately, when they move into the big leagues, these professionals often lack the knowledge, experience, tools, and skills to support the client's needs. They simply may not have what it takes to give advice on the multi-faceted needs of high-net-worth clients.

What You Don't Feel Can Kill You

Many wonder about the actual impact of adequate advice versus optimal advice. Well, consider the times you experienced a sudden, throbbing headache. Although you found the discomfort annoying, the pain is typically manageable with ibuprofen and some rest. You felt it, addressed it, and it passed without much consequence.

Compare such a headache to high blood pressure. Though we don't feel the numbers rise, the condition silently wreaks havoc on our bodies—our arteries narrow and ventricles thicken. With virtually no pressing symptoms, we increase our risk of heart disease, stroke, and other serious health issues. High blood pressure is the silent killer lurking beneath the surface, going unnoticed until it's too late.

But what if I told you a similar phenomenon lies hidden in the world of wealth management? Individuals with a higher net worth often have more complex financial needs. Yet, unlike a pounding headache, we don't necessarily feel the immediate effects of subpar financial advice.

Unfortunately, the difference between good and average advice can be subtle, almost imperceptible, at first. Small inefficiencies or missed opportunities may go unnoticed for years, seemingly harmless. But over time, these seemingly insignificant issues can compound, growing into significant problems or costs that impact our financial well-being and our future. Much like blood pressure—if we leave the advice we receive unchecked, the gradual damage it causes becomes more difficult to undo with each passing day.

Consider this: the overall management of your family's financial affairs may seem acceptable on the surface. But what if those results don't reflect the full potential of your situation? What if your portfolio could be more efficiently constructed to deliver higher returns relative to the amount of risk taken? What tax strategies could be employed to legally minimize your liabilities? What other strategies are available for your estate planning that could amplify your long-term legacy? The truth is that many of us unknowingly leave money on the table because we have not optimized our plans. A poorly constructed estate plan or business arrangement might not raise any red flags initially, but when complications arise down the road, it's often too late to remedy the situation.

The IRS isn't going to call us and say, "Hey, you could have saved a massive amount in taxes if you had structured your estate plan differently." It's up to us to seek the best advice and ensure we're making informed decisions about our finances. Unfortunately, inferior advice doesn't come with flashing red lights.

The Compounding Effect

As a financial advisor, I encounter common questions, 'Are a few minor inefficiencies in my investment, estate, or tax plans really such a big deal? Don't I have enough money now that I will be fine either way?" These are valid questions that may seem innocuous at first glance. After all, if a client already has significant wealth, how much difference can a small deviation really make?

Let me tell you, it can make all the difference in the world.

Imagine you're piloting a plane from Los Angeles to Las Vegas. Though confident in your direction, you accidentally set the navigation a mere five degrees off course. It shouldn't make much difference, right? The forty-five-minute drive from the Hoover Dam will be inconvenient but not devastating. On the other hand, if you're headed to New York, that same five-degree deviation will land you in Norfolk, Virginia, and if you happen to be heading to London, leave yourself plenty of time to travel there after you land in Geneva, Switzerland.

A five-degree error might not mean much initially, but the further you journey, the more that tiny deviation compounds. The more miles you need to travel, the greater the loss of time and money when you arrive at your destination.

Likewise, when you start with a higher degree of wealth, the smallest nuances in the way your wealth is managed can have a dramatic impact over time. Few advisors intentionally mislead clients; however, some just don't actually have the tools or experience to know the difference. And unfortunately, you may be getting advice from these professionals and not even realize it's less than you need. Those with substantial finances might not notice the difference because the mismanagement won't affect their lifestyle; however, like the cross-ocean effects of a five-degree miscalculation, these same people may find they have less to be generous with later in life than their counterparts who engaged a proper advisory team. Because wealth allows them to live comfortably, small inefficiencies in their financial strategies may not affect them on a day-to-day basis. However, staying comfortable doesn't equal optimal performance.

Most high-net-worth individuals have aspirations beyond their current level of comfort. They dream of second homes, retirement in luxury, supporting cherished charities, providing for their children and grandchildren, and leaving a lasting legacy. Yet, failing to fine-tune their financial plans can jeopardize these dreams.

Picture this: The difference between staying on course and deviating by even one degree could be the difference between realizing those dreams or falling short. The implications of these seemingly inconsequential deviations are staggering when compounded over time. Wealth management is rarely a short-term endeavor, and the compounding effect of inefficiencies over many years can be breathtaking. While you might be comfortable with an inferior wealth plan, you'll soon discover your retirement plans, aspirations of leaving bequests to favorite charities or funding your grandchildren's education could slip away as silently as the tide leaves the shore.

Settling for "comfortable" and "headed in the right direction" leads to average and less-than-average outcomes. Optimal should be the goal. "Good enough" should never be good enough when it comes to our financial futures. We must strive for precision, ensuring that every aspect of our wealth management plan is meticulously crafted to achieve our long-term objectives.

It is important to note that aiming for optimal doesn't mean you should be a "Monday-morning quarterback." Optimal simply controls the things in your power to control. This is not doing annual comparisons to determine if your advisor's investment selections performed "above average." Any intellectually honest advisor will tell you that predicting the future is impossible. This cannot be the goal. In fact, you would likely be best served to steer clear of those who seem to insinuate they have a crystal ball.

We suggest seeking optimal because we see the tremendous advantages of focusing on the tangible and measurable items. Proper asset allocation is measurable. Pre-tax strategies are clearly available in certain situations. The impacts of prudent estate planning can be precisely measured. The key is to focus on those items over which you have total control. The unpredictability of markets will always be present, but much more is well within our command.

The stakes are undeniably high for those with accumulated wealth. Small adjustments in financial strategies can yield substantial dividends over time. And no one wants their financial plan to be one degree off course, not when they understand the potential long-term consequences. The realization of missed opportunities should serve as a powerful motivator to recalibrate our financial strategies and move toward precision in wealth management.

In the end, we need an advisor who recognizes that the smallest adjustments today can lead to monumental differences tomorrow. Aiming for optimization gives our wealth the best opportunity to serve as a catalyst for realizing our deepest aspirations.

In the following pages, I want you to see how informed choices and strategic adjustments can profoundly impact the financial trajectory of the affluent. If you've amassed significant wealth and find yourself navigating the complexities and opportunities that lie ahead alone, consider this book your compass. Let's chart a course to bring hope to your horizon. This comprehensive approach to wealth management involves assembling the right team of advisors to accompany you and help you identify and eliminate inefficiencies in your financial strategy. Together, we'll navigate the complex landscape of wealth management and ensure you make the most of your resources. Let's explore the thoughtful approach of our solution, *The Efficient Family Office*.

2

The Evolution of Wealth Management in the Digital Age

I can't help but marvel at the whirlwind of changes technology has brought into our lives. Not long ago, the mere thought of summoning a ride with a tap on our phones or ordering groceries with a few clicks seemed like a distant dream. Yet here we are, living in a world where technological innovation has seamlessly integrated into almost every aspect of our daily routines.

But amidst the convenience and abundance of information these advances bring, one profound transformation has gone unnoticed—the evolution of financial advice in the digital age. Few truly realize how technological advancements have fundamentally reshaped the way top advisors approach wealth management.

The Impact of Technology on Wealth Management

More than a decade ago, visionary entrepreneurs recognized the potential for technology to streamline and enhance the wealth management process. They heralded "robo-advisors" as the future of financial planning and personal portfolio management. Automated, technology-only platforms promised efficiency and convenience, offering algorithm-driven solutions to investors at a fraction of the cost of traditional advisors.

Yet, time proved that while technology effectively optimized certain aspects of financial management, particularly that of portfolio construction, implementation, monitoring, and rebalancing, it couldn't replace the human touch. Finances are deeply intertwined with a person's unique emotions, aspirations, and fears—aspects unmeasurable by artificial intelligence. The industry discovered humans needed more than a cold, mechanical system to manage their finances— they craved personal connection, guidance, and reassurance.

The rise and fall of the hype surrounding robo-advisors reminded us of a valuable insight: technology can enhance efficiency; however, the human element brings immeasurable value to wealth management. Automated algorithms will never be enough; human beings seek understanding, empathy, and someone they can trust.

Despite its short-lived popularity, technology-driven financial advice left a powerful legacy. The era of robo-advisors paved the way for a new paradigm in financial services. The tools and technologies developed during that time found their place within large institutions as well as boutique firms, revolutionizing the way advisors interact with their clients.

Today, this cutting-edge technology streamlines and optimizes a number of tasks central to portfolio management and reporting. Technology, once feared as a disruptor, has become our greatest ally, a valuable tool in the hands of human advisors—men and women whose wisdom and expertise we recognize as crucial to the process. Rather than replacing advisors with machines, we empower them with ever-evolving and increasingly powerful tools, revolutionizing the way they serve their clients.

We Can Leverage Technology or Squander It

Technological innovation has certainly changed the arena of our everyday lives. Even octogenarians rely on cell phones and streaming services. And we order everything online today—groceries, medicine, furniture, and more. With just a few clicks, we have a ride from the airport and a hotel or a beach house for the week. Appointment scheduling, dinner reservations, and even virtual healthcare services have made life a great deal easier. Still, some resist the change. And while, in most instances, leaving things entirely to humans is a feasible option, it can be quite costly in the world of wealth management.

Technological advancements have taken processes that once consumed hours of laborious paperwork and manual calculations and streamlined them to the click of a button. Advisors can analyze data more efficiently, deliver insights with unprecedented speed, and execute transactions faster and easier than ever before.

Many firms saw the technology as a means to simplify internal efforts and bolster profits while maintaining the status quo. Efficiency became synonymous with self-preservation,

and they confined innovation to optimizing internal operations. With advanced options at their fingertips, these
advisors chose to continue their services of investing money,
doing basic planning, and scheduling periodic meetings. They
provided the bare minimums, the table stakes in the world
of wealth management. Thriving in their comfort zones,
these firms squandered the opportunities afforded by digital
advancements and became content with the notion that good
enough was, well, good enough.

At the same time, another breed of firms, a minority
among the masses, saw technology as a catalyst for change
and better service rather than a means to an end. These vision-
aries became pioneers in their field. They dared to challenge
the status quo and redefine the role of wealth management
in the digital age. These advisors understood true value lies
in the extras, the added layers of service and expertise that
differentiate the ordinary from the extraordinary.

Kathmere rose to become one among those few who stood
out. We recognized that efficiency should not be hoarded but
shared, and the benefits of technology should flow back to
those who mattered most: our clients. We opted for greater
than simply streamlining our processes and calling it a day.
We saw an opportunity to do more and be more for those
who entrusted us with their financial futures.

Thus, *The Efficient Family Office* was born—a testament
to our commitment to innovation and client-centricity. We
didn't stop at automating tasks or cutting costs. Instead, we
reinvested those savings into enhancing our services, expand-
ing our team, and deepening our expertise.

Recognizing the importance of holistic wealth management beyond just investments, we leveraged the technology
and welcomed estate and tax attorney experience into our
ranks. We sought out exclusive private investment opportunities so we could offer our clients access to avenues previously

reserved for the elite. Our revamped reporting systems allowed us to provide comprehensive insights into every facet of our clients' financial lives, even those we didn't directly manage.

But perhaps most importantly, we fostered stronger connections with our clients' broader financial team. We understood that collaboration between CPAs, attorneys, and other financial institutions was key to unlocking true wealth management, and we spared no effort in bridging the gap between siloed advisors.

Technological advancements continue to evolve daily. They force every high-net-worth individual to stand at a vital crossroads. They must face the imperative to demand more and expect more from their wealth management firms. Otherwise, they squander opportunities and allow the compounding effects of inefficiency to rob them of their legacy.

Ironically, the firms that expanded their services, built exceptional teams, and became laser-focused on client satisfaction remained competitively priced, sometimes even less expensive than their peers. The speed of technology allows them to offer additional layers of service without significantly changing their fee schedule. It's a misconception to assume that getting more value from your advisor has to come at a higher cost.

If you learn nothing else from my message, I hope you never again settle for mediocrity or tolerate complacency. Look for an advisory firm that embraces change and harnesses technology—not for their gain but for yours.

Now, let's delve into the implications of this technological revolution for advisors and clients alike. I want to equip you with the knowledge to identify an elite firm that aligns with your needs—a firm that offers multiple layers of service and possesses the unique capabilities of The Efficient Family Office.

3

The Four Silent Killers

As we already discussed, the effects of sub-optimal advice can be as unfelt and detrimental to your finances as high blood pressure is to your health. And though I've already mentioned a few situations that can adversely affect your finances, the four scenarios I list in this chapter are prominent examples of what I would call four "silent killers" of the future potential of your wealth.

Killer #1 – The Wealth Advisor Who Isn't

In the professional world, titles hold weight. They convey expertise, experience, and trust. Consider the titles of doctor or lawyer. These designations require rigorous education and testing.

On the other hand, becoming an investment advisor requires no mandatory coursework. You don't even need a high school diploma. The only real requirement, the Series 65, is an exam that can be passed with a modest amount of preparation. This test doesn't focus on the fundamentals of financial planning or tax or investments. It primarily tests your knowledge of securities law, which is of little value in wealth management practice.

Despite the lack of educational requirements, the financial advisory world boasts titles as abundant as stars in the sky. Yet, much like those distant celestial bodies, they often lack substance. Firms toss around terms like wealth advisor, financial planner, private client group, and investment advisor interchangeably. With blurring lines of distinction, the labels become mere placeholders, leaving clients confused about the true expertise and capabilities of those who wield them.

The titles plastered on business cards and office doors offer scant insight into the depth of knowledge a financial advisor truly possesses. Unlike professions with more defined standards and qualifications, the financial advisory realm operates in a nebulous realm where titles speak more to marketing than merit. As a result, individuals with vastly different skill sets and breadths of service all lay claim to the same generic designations.

Throughout my career, I've encountered countless self-proclaimed wealth advisors. Unfortunately, many specialize in narrow niches of the financial industry or focus solely on investment selection, while others do nothing more than sell life insurance or annuities. And, though all those areas have an importance of their own, each presents a small piece of the financial puzzle. When we examine the wide array of opportunities and unique complexities of those with high net worth, we realize the discrepancy between title and practice leaves clients vulnerable to a whole host of issues.

For clients with substantial wealth, comprehensive wealth management is paramount. Narrow advice poses a significant risk. At this level, they require strategic guidance in areas such as estate planning, tax strategy, charitable giving, and legacy distribution. Failing to address these critical components can have far-reaching consequences, jeopardizing the financial security of affluent families.

So, what distinguishes a genuine wealth advisor from their superficial counterparts? It's not merely about picking investments or selling insurance policies. A true wealth advisor transcends the roles of investment selection and insurance policies. At the heart of a valuable wealth advisory relationship lies a commitment to understanding and addressing the diverse needs of affluent families. This encompasses everything from crafting individualized investment strategies to devising comprehensive estate plans. A worthy wealth advisor serves as a steward of their clients' financial legacies, guiding them through the intricacies of wealth preservation and distribution.

In the journey toward financial prosperity, the guidance of a trusted advisor is invaluable. Yet, amidst the sea of titles, clarity demands due diligence. Clients need to give themselves permission to scrutinize the credentials and expertise of prospective advisors to ensure the firms they choose align with their comprehensive wealth management needs.

A Word about the Alphabet Soup of Designations

As we mentioned, the world of financial advising offers a variety of titles and acronyms to tack behind a professional's name. Deciphering these designations can feel like navigating a maze. Understanding the difference is crucial for anyone seeking reliable financial advice.

The Gold Standards

Among the plethora of financial advisor designations, a few stand out as benchmarks of excellence and dedication. These titles require extensive education, experience, and ongoing professional development. Here are some of the most prestigious:

Certified Financial Planner (CFP®)

The CFP® designation stands as one of the most recognized and respected in the financial planning industry. Advisors with this credential have completed a comprehensive course of study, passed a rigorous examination, and adhered to a strict code of ethics. CFP professionals have several years of experience and extensive training to help clients with a broad array of financial needs, from retirement planning to tax strategies.

Chartered Financial Analyst (CFA)

The highly esteemed CFA designation requires passing three levels of exams, which cover topics such as investment analysis, portfolio management, and ethical standards. Each level demands hundreds of hours of study. CFAs typically fill roles involving investment research, fund management, and asset allocation. Their deep understanding of financial markets makes them invaluable to serious investors.

Juris Doctor (JD) and Master of Laws (LLM)

Legal expertise can be crucial in financial advising, particularly in areas like estate planning and tax law. A JD indicates that an advisor has graduated from law school, while an LLM signifies advanced legal training, often in a specialized field like taxation. Advisors with these credentials bring a deep understanding of legal intricacies, which can be critical for clients who need complex financial and legal advice.

Certified Public Accountant (CPA)

CPA is synonymous with expertise in accounting and tax preparation. To receive the designation, one must pass a demanding examination and meet specific educational and experience requirements. CPAs help clients navigate complex tax laws and provide strategic tax planning. Individuals and businesses aiming to optimize their tax situation find their skills invaluable.

The Illusions

Not all financial advisor designations carry the same weight. Some credentials require little more than a fee and attending a short course and suggest a level of expertise that may not exist. The ultimate message is that you should not assume that letters at the end of a business card or an email signature are the result of years of study and hard work.

Beware of Financial Advisor Awards

In addition to designations, those looking for an advisor need to be on the lookout for those professionals who boast awards. Like those titles and acronyms, awards may not be a good indication of competence. In fact, the majority of awards could be considered bogus, paid marketing tools.

I read an article that demonstrated the depth of the award problem. It highlighted a financial planner named Max Tailwag'er, who had been nominated to Medical Economics Magazine's 2013 list of Best Financial Advisors for Doctors. Since Max was named as a top financial planner in the 2009 "Guide to America's Top Financial Planners," this wasn't a total surprise.

The author of the article, Allan Roth, included a picture of Mr. Tailwag'er with his award. He explained that when the notice of the acknowledgment came to his office, he saw through the "prestigious award" presented by SLD Industries. His first instinct was to throw away the invitation, but curious as to how far they would carry their charade, he filled out the form with his dog's name. Since Max had no credit card, Mr. Roth had to send the money, and in just a couple of weeks, Max's award arrived.

Yes, the Consumers' Research Council of America Planners award was bestowed on a dog.

Obviously, this award and others like it require little more than a pulse and a checkbook. Allan Roth's article isn't the only one that exposes these trivial awards that require payments.

Another investment advisor exposed a similar award given in Atlanta in his blog. Apparently, to be named to *Atlanta* magazine's Five Star Wealth Manager list, you simply have to be employed as an advisor, have a "favorable regulatory and complaint history review," and be willing to accept new clients. Basically, if you aren't too big of a crook, you win the award.

These misleading "best of" lists are not unique to the financial advice industry. But similar lists for lawyers, surgeons, dermatologists, and dentists include men and women who have completed lengthy schooling and passed arduous exams.

Other awards may simply rank advisors based on "size of business," which should also not be the measuring stick of the quality of an advisor. Admittedly, we have appeared on some of those lists because Kathmere Capital is a sizable firm at this point in 2024. However, make no mistake about my message. Those lists do not know anything about your business. They have not been in your client meetings or seen your recommendations, and they don't understand the level of depth, expertise, or service capabilities of the team. The size of a business is, at least, a better measurement than a paid advertisement like some other awards, but it is still by no means the method by which an advisor should be judged.

This means consumers face a real dilemma. The field of wealth management has tarnished itself with the loose qualifications and bogus accolades. If you can't trust industry rankings or certifications, how can you feel comfortable allowing someone to handle your assets?

It is imperative for those searching for an advisor to do their due diligence and unmask the wealth advisor who isn't. By sticking with those few accredited designations and ignoring awards and other fluff achievements, clients can safeguard their financial futures and embark on a path toward true wealth stewardship. By the end of this book, you will be in a far better position to ask the right questions and feel confident that you can tell the difference between an amateur and a professional.

Killer #2 - You've Outgrown Your Advisor

I have good news and bad news. The good news is you've reached many of your financial goals. You may have done it through years of saving, building your business, stock options, or you accumulated your wealth in another way. Perhaps you're managing an inheritance from parents or grandparents. Regardless, your stable financial situation has put you in a comfortable position. The bad news is the financial advisor who helped with your early investments may no longer be a good fit.

We know this might be a tough one to swallow. If you've worked with an advisor for many years, you've likely built a relationship based on trust and shared goals. However, with an evolving financial situation, needs become more complex, and goals expand. Sometimes, the financial advisor who helped you rise to this place isn't equipped to handle the new demands.

I liken this difficult decision to the role of a primary care physician. For many years, a primary care physician is perfectly suited to address a patient's health concerns. From routine check-ups to managing minor ailments, they play a pivotal role in maintaining good health and provide valuable guidance on preventive measures.

However, as individuals progress through different stages of life, their healthcare needs evolve. If a patient requires bypass surgery or develops cancer, the primary care physician takes a back seat to cardiologists, oncologists, and surgeons.

Understanding when to transition from a generalist to a specialist is key to ensuring optimal care and outcomes, and this truth applies to wealth management as much as it does to health care. By embracing this analogy for their wealth management needs, individuals can make informed decisions about their financial health and access the specialized expertise needed to navigate the complexities of wealth accumulation and preservation.

Making this move has nothing to do with the intention or effort that an advisor puts forth in doing their best; it's simply a recognition that your needs may have outgrown their capabilities. Many advisors specialize in helping clients in the accumulation phase. Like general physicians, these advisors excel at the basics—helping to establish and articulate clear goals and tracking progress towards those goals, developing and implementing simple portfolio strategies, and providing basic financial, tax, and estate planning advice. However, strategies change when you reach the next level of wealth. You might assume your advisor will just use the same process to manage a larger number. But truthfully, there may be a certain line in the sand where your current advisor may not have the expertise, tools, or team required to guide you effectively.

Outgrowing your advisor comes with a host of realities. First, an advisor accustomed to working with smaller portfolios might not have access to or the necessary skills and experience to properly evaluate the investment vehicles and strategies necessary to optimize your returns and manage your risk effectively. Second, your current advisor may lack the expertise or experience to navigate the complexities of your financial situation. High net-worth planning needs someone who understands the intricacies of estate planning, tax optimization, and wealth preservation strategies. Your current advisor may not have the knowledge or resources to navigate these waters effectively.

Furthermore, there's the question of a team. As your financial needs become more complex, a team of specialists may be necessary to address them adequately. This could include estate attorneys, high-level investment analysts, tax experts, and more. Many hardworking advisors claim they can work with your current advisors to make sure the plan comes together. That may sound good in theory. However, a wealth advisor sitting at the center of a client's financial life who lacks knowledge on key topics will ultimately lead to a plan that breaks down over time.

Finally, it's important to consider alignment. Does your current advisor's firm have a structure and philosophy that aligns with your new reality? Too often, loyalty to a longtime advisor—someone we consider a friend and confidante—will cause us to try to fit a square peg into a round hole. Compromise could cost you dearly.

Depending on the specifics of your financial situation, it might be possible to keep your current advisor while bringing in additional advisory expertise to address your evolving needs. Occasionally, the original advisor can continue to manage a portion of a client's portfolio while a new advisor implements a more comprehensive strategy like The Efficient Family Office for the remainder. Nevertheless, when you reach this point, it's vital to acknowledge the difficulty of the situation without letting sentimentality cloud your judgment. The benefits of finding an advisor who can truly serve your new reality far outweigh the discomfort of making a change.

If you've accumulated significant wealth and your financial situation has become more complex, it's crucial to ensure your advisor is still the right fit for you. And while it might be tempting to ask your current advisor if they are equipped to handle your new circumstances, their answer may not be entirely objective. You can likely expect any advisor to say they are up to the task of managing your more complex situation. The successful execution of that role could be questionable if it is not their typical client profile. Later, in Chapter 7, I offer a number of specific questions that you can ask to help you discern whether or not a given advisor is up to the task.

One way to gauge your advisor's specialization and niche is by examining their website. Pay attention to the language they use and the content they provide. Advisors often tailor their web pages to their target clients. If the content or language used no longer aligns with your needs, that's an initial sign that your advisor might not be the right fit anymore.

Another approach is to review their regulatory disclosures and reporting, which can often be found on the Securities and Exchange Commission's Investment Advisor Public Disclosure website. These documents can reveal valuable information about their focus and specialization. You can also inquire about additional services offered to clients at your new level of wealth. If you don't notice a discernible difference from your current experience, your advisor may not be equipped to handle your newfound complexity.

You can also ask your advisor about his or her experience in reporting, coordinating, and summarizing a household's entire portfolio, not merely the assets they manage directly. If the advisor doesn't have a readily available reporting suite that demonstrates their proficiency in managing both their portfolios and external ones, it's a clear indication that they may not be prepared for the demands of your new financial picture.

Selecting a new advisor when you've outgrown your current one can be challenging. At Kathmere, we encourage prospective clients to look for their Right Fit Advisor—someone who can handle all their financial scenarios based on the amount they can afford to invest as well as the size of the accounts they have to manage.

The conundrum of outgrowing your advisor is probably one of the more challenging aspects of wealth accumulation. These professionals often become our friends. And the relationship might expand into social aspects and beyond. Regardless, loyalty alone must never keep us from asking the critical questions, evaluating our needs, and considering the needed changes to optimize our financial plan.

Killer #3 - The Mess of Multiple Voices

In my financial planning career, one of the first lessons I learned was the importance of diversification. It's a principle preached by every seasoned investor: don't put all your eggs in one basket. The strategy encourages us to spread our wealth across different assets to minimize risk. This strategy is generally a very good idea as it relates to the overall investment of your assets. However, some clients take the strategy of diversification in directions that may be counterproductive.

Clients with more significant wealth are often tempted to also diversify with multiple advisors. Diversification of assets is clearly the right logic, so why not also diversify with multiple advisors assisting you? At first glance, the approach appears to offer some benefits. Different perspectives have the potential to bring several unique investment opportunities or strategies to the table. Many find comfort in knowing multiple experts oversee their financial affairs.

It sounds so logical. However, as time progresses, cracks usually begin to show. Most of the time, the distinct lack of coordination results in a fragmented approach to wealth management. Because each advisor operates within their own narrow, self-contained lane, they remain oblivious to what the others are doing. It becomes like trying to solve a puzzle with pieces scattered across multiple tables—a recipe for confusion and missed opportunities.

In my experience, there are three main pitfalls that come with working with multiple advisors with no clear quarterback or coordinator in place:

1. Disjointed and Inefficient Portfolio Management

In reality, while diversification may have its merits as an investment strategy, it doesn't often make sense to diversify the advisors themselves other than in very rare circumstances. As you can see, it leads to a unique set of challenges. When someone accumulates significant wealth and decides to entrust it to multiple individuals or entities, they unwittingly assume the role of the wealth advisor themselves.

Imagine you have a substantial sum of money, and you decide to divide it between two advisors. Each advisor has his or her own strategy and investment approach. Over time, they come to you with a host of divergent ideas and proposals for your money. Suddenly, you, the client, find yourself in the position of wealth strategist. In essence, though you're paying others to help you make the most of your wealth, you've become responsible for finalizing the decisions on crucial financial options. Instead of advisors taking charge and guiding the ship, you become the offensive coordinator, a task for which few are qualified.

It is also worth considering whether dividing assets amongst two advisors will necessarily produce the added impact of diversification as one would hope. Take, for example, a person with two advisors, each of whom invests in nearly the same portfolio. While there may be the appearance of diversification, in reality, it has accomplished almost nothing in terms of actually diversifying, reducing risk, or introducing unique ideas.

2. Tax Inefficiencies

Perhaps the most egregious drawback is the inability to effectively engage in tax strategies across accounts. Assets scattered among different advisors make it nearly impossible to coordinate tax planning efforts. Opportunities for tax loss harvesting, strategic asset location, and other tax-saving strategies slip through the cracks and cost valuable dollars in unnecessary taxes. The higher a person's net worth, the bigger this planning opportunity becomes and the more it can impact the results.

3. Fee Inefficiencies

Working with multiple advisors also has the potential to invite the issue of fee inefficiencies. With wealth spread across several firms, people often pay redundant fees for similar services. The leak in the financial bucket slowly drains wealth without the client even realizing it. And, to add insult to injury, this philosophy steals the opportunity for fee optimizations that come with consolidating assets. Usually, the more a client has with one firm, the lower the fees will be to manage the aggregate portfolio. By spreading these assets across many different firms, it is possible that each advisor is charging a fee much higher than the aggregate portfolio amount should be paying.

In some cases, a glimmer of hope can be found amidst the chaos—a solution to the mess of multiple voices. It comes in the form of appointing a "Lead Advisor." This shifts the burden of management from the client to the capable hands of a single individual.

The lead advisor acts as the quarterback of the financial team, overseeing the entire portfolio and coordinating efforts across all accounts. With this person's expertise and guidance, inefficiencies can be minimized, and you can begin to see alignment in the overall financial affairs.

To illustrate further, let me share the story of Julie and Stewart, a couple who spent years diligently building their wealth. Hard work and wise investing gave them the hope of a comfortable future for themselves and their family. So, as their wealth grew, they felt the weight of making sure it was managed well.

Julie and Stewart found multiple financial advisors who promised to guide them toward financial success. Diversifying their advisors seemed to make sense because they didn't want to "risk it with one advisor," and both people seemed smart. With a variety of perspectives and strategies from trained experts, it seemed like a prudent approach—a way to safeguard their wealth against unforeseen risks.

However, as time passed, Julie and Stewart began to experience a tangled web of confusion and inefficiency. Each advisor operated in isolation, so the advice they received for investment strategies often conflicted. Each meeting focused on only one piece of their overall financial picture. They discovered missed opportunities and suboptimal outcomes too far after the fact to help.

The fee inefficiencies, along with other disjointed disadvantages, became a drain on their resources. These eroded their potential wealth without them realizing it for a number of years. But the thing that finally sent them searching for another alternative was their struggle to coordinate tax strategies. As they watched their tax bill grow larger with each passing year, Julie and Stewart began to question their approach to financial planning. They longed for clarity and direction, and they knew their multi-advisor strategy wasn't the solution.

They realized they had a few alternatives to fix this mess. First, they could determine if one of the two existing advisors was capable of meeting the needs they so desperately recognized. If so, they could consolidate with them and make their situation more fee efficient, as well as make it easier to manage tax strategies and overall household investment strategy.

A second option was to seek a completely new advisor—someone who ran a version of The Efficient Family Office and consolidated with them to capture all of the benefits they weren't enjoying in their current state.

The last option was a Kathmere concept we call the "Lead Advisor Role." We will talk more about this idea later in the book, but it is an ideal solution for the client who feels that multiple advisors is still a good idea but doesn't want to be the person in charge of the whole situation (The Mess of Multiple Voices).

The Lead Advisor is simply one of the advisors on the team, but this advisor comes with an entirely different set of expectations and responsibilities. Instead of just managing the portion of wealth that the client has entrusted to them, they take a broader and far more holistic role. They are in charge of knowing, understanding, and reporting on the entire HOUSEHOLD, not just the assets they manage. When one of the advisors has an idea or a recommendation, the Lead Advisor role is included in making sure it is a cohesive and prudent strategy for the client's overall picture. (As you can imagine, Kathmere has fully developed our ability to serve in the Lead Advisor role, and it is a meaningful offering to those clients who need this additional support. More to come on this in Chapter 6).

Your wealth requires holistic and comprehensive oversight, not piecemeal account management. While it may sound daunting, entrusting a single financial advisor with the management of your entire portfolio can offer numerous advantages. Lower fees, more access to investments with minimum investment amounts, and greater tax efficiency top the list. Most importantly, your financial strategy will be crystal clear to both you and your chosen advisor, and clarity will add tremendous peace to your life.

The risks associated with multiple advisors operating independently, unaware of each other's actions, are more significant than many clients might realize. This lack of coordination can undermine even the best-intentioned wealth management strategies, leaving clients exposed to unnecessary risks and missed opportunities. Clarity, communication, and coordination are invaluable in the world of finance. Kathmere's *Efficient Family Office* seeks to inject this trifecta into the management of your wealth.

Killer #4 – Estate Planning Disarray

As a financial advisor, I often find myself navigating through the intricate webs of investment strategies, tax planning, and retirement goals with my clients. These "fun" conversations fill our days, and we readily engage in them armed with spreadsheets and projections to aid our discussions about their big goals and dreams. But another topic lurks in the shadows, one we skirt around or often prefer to avoid—estate planning.

I understand the reasons behind our hesitancy. The proverbial elephant in the room of financial discussions makes most people uncomfortable. Our inevitable end is a reality we prefer to ignore. No one wants to dwell on mortality when we can analyze markets and manage portfolios.

Despite its lack of popularity, estate planning stands as one of the most crucial aspects of financial stewardship. This blueprint shapes our legacy and impacts generations. Done right, estate planning can ensure our hard-earned wealth is preserved and distributed according to our wishes. Neglected, it can unravel even the most carefully constructed financial plans.

Sadly, I've witnessed the ramifications of assuming estate planning is a one-and-done deal. Clients diligently execute their estate documents, ticking off boxes on their to-do list, then they promptly tuck them away on a shelf or in a drawer, where they gather dust alongside forgotten trinkets. The initial sense of accomplishment fades, and the pressing demands of everyday life push this important aspect of financial planning to the recesses of the client's memory, brought to light only fleetingly when the topic resurfaces in conversation or circumstance.

I've seen the pattern repeated time and again. Even the most skilled estate attorneys have no way to keep up with the ongoing maintenance of family dynamics, evolving net worth, or the ever-shifting landscape of how tax laws will impact each one of their clients. Their job is to draft the documents to best fit your life picture in the moment, not to ensure their continued relevance in the face of life's twists and turns.

Meanwhile, most "typical" advisors, from CPAs to financial planners, possess a mere cursory knowledge of their clients' estate plans and the needs associated. They make certain your wills, trusts, and powers of attorney exist, but beyond that, they simply are not equipped to evaluate the legal intricacies of the estate plan. Left to these well-intentioned professionals, the gap widens between intention and execution, leaving clients vulnerable to the disconnect between their evolving financial situation, ever-changing family profile, and whatever the prior documents said when they were executed.

We work with many clients who executed their legal documents long before they came our way. They worked with competent estate planners who tailored their plans to meet their needs at the time of drafting. We rarely encounter an estate attorney incapable of drafting estate plans suitable for the needs of the client at a certain moment in time. Unfortunately, the disarray happens in the shadows long after the documents have been filed.

Estate planning negligence becomes particularly glaring for those who have moved from the young family at the beginning of their accumulation phase into the stage of a high-net-worth individual. As assets grow and families expand, estates rise to a greater level of complexity. Most clients don't remember the precise instructions in their first draft. In fact, most would say they don't remember what they decided within a week of its completion. The need to regularly scrutinize estate plans transforms into a preeminent assignment. Yet, all too often, this essential step falls by the wayside, overshadowed by more immediate concerns.

This is where the divide between traditional wealth advisors and innovative firms becomes starkly apparent. While most financial planners offer little more than a box to check when it comes to estate planning, a select few go the extra mile to ensure this vital document remains integrated into the broader financial plan. These firms recognize the interconnectedness of wealth management and estate preservation, refusing to treat them as distinct silos. In other words, the question "Do you have wills and other legal documents in place?" does not lead to a conversation that will add meaningful impact to the planning process.

At the forefront of this movement stands The Efficient Family Office. At Kathmere, we refuse to leave estate planning to an afterthought. Rather, we make it a cornerstone of our approach. Our team works alongside dedicated specialists to ensure that the estate planning evolves and changes to reflect the ongoing needs of the family. By embedding estate planning into the fabric of our services, we ensure the plan for a legacy remains a living, breathing part of each of our client's financial journeys. This ongoing dialogue and coordination between the wealth advisory team and estate attorney creates a robust estate strategy as well as a well-rounded wealth management plan that can yield concrete outcomes.

These outcomes vary from prudent asset protection, special needs considerations, estate equalization, and certainly tax minimization—all important and worthwhile objectives that can help a family to achieve significant financial goals across multiple generations.

It is worth noting that part of the unique value that top firms provide is not only asking about estate planning and making it part of the planning process but also having the in-house expertise to advise accordingly. As part of The Efficient Family Office process, the team from Kathmere has an estate and tax attorney who is part of the team. While we are not practicing law and not drafting documents, this advanced level of expertise is very rare and provides clients with a high-level sounding board as they explore the potential needs of their ever-evolving estate plan. Other firms may speak of their involvement in estate and tax matters but not have the expertise to actually deliver high-level advice. It would be wise for the client to understand the difference when considering potential firms.

In the end, the success of any wealth advisory firm should never be measured by simple investment returns or tax savings but by the enduring legacy it helps clients build. In a world where estate plans too often get relegated to the annals of forgotten paperwork, those firms that rise to the challenge stand head and shoulders above the rest. By adopting The Efficient Family Office model, clients can ensure their estate plan remains relevant and aligned with their evolving circumstances and desires.

4

What Is a Family Office?

The term "family office" comes surrounded by a veil of mystery and intrigue. Yet, behind these buzzwords lies a concept grounded in practicality and efficiency. The family office has its roots in the in-house businesses established by ultra-high-net-worth families at the beginning of the Industrial Revolution with the singular purpose of managing their personal wealth.

Imagine a family able to manage their wealth any way they see fit. Every move they make is geared toward what they believe is in their best interests. Without cost considerations, they have a simple goal—to optimize the end result. What would be the advantages, and how could one family make it happen?

The Family Office structure came out of this question. And the result was a family assembling a team of primarily internal experts dedicated solely to their financial affairs. These in-house professionals often include tax advisors, estate attorneys, and investment professionals, as well as close relationships with external advisors, including insurance specialists and banking advisors, all of whom are working tirelessly on the family's best interests. They spend one hundred percent of their energy searching for investment opportunities and addressing their employer's diverse financial needs across each of the key areas of wealth management.

But the scope of services doesn't end there for the family offices of old. In addition to the core financial roles, a family office may help to support and provide concierge services, ranging from airline travel arrangements and property management to bill payment assistance and reservations for tickets and restaurants. These personalized services catered to the unique lifestyle demands of ultra-high-net-worth families, ensuring seamless management of both their financial and non-financial affairs.

So why would these ultra-high-net-worth families opt to establish a family office instead of relying on external advisors? Over time, these families recognized the value of handpicking the best and brightest professionals and bringing them in-house to focus exclusively on their unique needs.

Yes, they could certainly have enlisted many of the best and brightest from external advisory firms all over the world. However, those individuals would also serve the interests of many other families and institutions. This lack of true internal collaboration is where much of the traditional advisory structure breaks down for these families, making the Family Office structure so attractive.

The effectiveness of the family office transcends the mere presence of internal experts. It lies in the collaboration and coordination of the entire family balance sheet and financial strategies. The family office parallels having a team of personal physicians. Imagine a cardiologist, gastroenterologist, primary care doctor, and dermatologist all working under one roof solely dedicated to your family's health. The level of precision and oversight would be unparalleled. In essence, the family office financial structure mirrors this model.

By consolidating all financial functions under one roof, the family office facilitates seamless coordination among specialists, eliminating the disjointed and all too common poorly coordinated financial strategies we sampled in the "Four Silent Killers." The family office represents more than just a luxurious perk for ultra-high-net-worth families—it's a strategic imperative. The family office empowers these upper-echelon families to navigate the complexities of their wealth with precision and efficiency.

Success Leaves Clues

We all understand that certain benefits stem from considerable wealth. It gives the ultra-wealthy the freedom to design systems and structures that cater precisely to their needs. Still, as I have explored the intricacies of wealth management and the unique ability of the ultra-wealthy to shape the management of their financial resources according to their preferences, I've discovered a simple yet profound truth: successful individuals tend to follow certain patterns and practices.

The concept of the family office gives us just one example. Far more than only physical office space, it represents a sophisticated approach to managing wealth—a manifestation of deliberate planning and strategic decision-making. At its core, the family office embodies the pinnacle of cohesive financial management, where every facet of wealth stewardship is carefully orchestrated to achieve optimal outcomes.

The emphasis on integration distinguishes the family office from conventional wealth management approaches.

Taxes play a significant role in wealth management, and the ultra-wealthy understand the importance of proactive tax planning. Within the family office framework, tax professionals work hand in hand with investment advisors and legal experts to structure investments and other transactions in the most tax-efficient manner. By leveraging their expertise, they minimize tax liabilities and maximize after-tax returns, ensuring that every financial decision aligns with the family's overall tax strategy.

Estate planning plays a critical role in the family office structure. Ultra-high net-worth individuals have an even greater stake in preserving wealth for future generations. Estate planning professionals within the family office collaborate closely with legal and tax experts to develop comprehensive plans tailored to the family's unique needs and objectives. From establishing trusts to implementing succession plans, they ensure the family's assets are protected and transferred efficiently while minimizing tax implications and preserving wealth for future generations.

The family office may also support someone who facilitates insurance needs. With jewelry, homes, cars, and collectibles, the act of protecting so many valuable assets could become overwhelming. The multiple types of insurance, the ways they pay out, and how they interact with taxes and investments demand extensive research. On top of that, most of these high-net-worth families control several businesses and non-profits that require specialized insurance.

Investment professionals obviously play a central role within the family office ecosystem. Tasked with managing the family's portfolio, they work in tandem with tax and legal advisors to design investment strategies that align with the family's goals and risk tolerance. Through diligent research, strategic asset allocation, and ongoing monitoring, investment experts aim to generate attractive risk-adjusted returns while mitigating downside risk. Some assets may be managed internally by Family Office staff, while others might be externally managed by niche asset managers. Regardless of whether the funds are managed internally or externally, all investments are coordinated and considered by the Family Office team. Nothing ever happens in a vacuum within a Family Office structure.

Finally, operational professionals oversee the day-to-day management of the family's financial affairs—from bill payment and cash flow management to coordinating with external service providers. By centralizing these operational functions within the family office, they streamline processes, enhance efficiency, and provide the family with a single point of contact for all their financial and cash management needs.

The family office represents a holistic approach to wealth management. By unifying professionals from diverse disciplines and fostering collaboration across departments, the family office ensures that every financial decision is made with a comprehensive understanding of its implications on taxes, estate planning, investments, and operations, as well as the personal plans and milestones of the family.

Establishing a dedicated family office may not be feasible for all but the wealthiest individuals and their families; however, everyone can benefit from the principles it embodies. By adopting an integrated approach to wealth management and leveraging the expertise of trusted advisors, individuals can achieve similar levels of sophistication and effectiveness in managing their finances.

Therefore, to maximize the effectiveness of the family office, rather than replicate the entity in its entirety, innovative firms like Kathmere have chosen to emulate the core principles and benefits of the traditional family office. Revolutionizing wealth management, The Efficient Family Office recognizes the value of integration and collaboration and affords high net-worth individuals a team of trusted advisors and professionals ready to provide advice, solutions, and reporting tailored to the needs of a broader audience.

The Efficient Family Office Provides Everything You Need

Establishing and maintaining a Family Office entails significant costs the average high-net-worth client can't sustain. Nevertheless, focusing on the elements of the Family Office most relevant to eliminating inefficiencies and maximizing strategic output is a very worthwhile effort. By pulling out the most essential elements of the Family Office's financial advisory team, we can accomplish similar results:

- *Cash Flow Planning* is a fundamental need for even the most simple financial situation.
- *Investment Management* activities are vital whether you have accumulated significant liquid assets or are beginning to build your wealth.
- *Tax Planning* is important whether you are just starting to accumulate wealth or are Elon Musk.
- A good *Estate Plan* is as important for you as it is for Jeff Bezos. It might be a smaller number, but maximizing legacy and protecting assets from risk and from creditors is important at any level.
- *Risk Management and Insurance* is critical regardless of your level of wealth.
- *Retirement Planning* also affects almost every level of financial complexity. Few realize the benefits or the intricacies involved in contributing to your own tax-favored retirement plans. There are better and worse ways to structure these plans, and as we said before, the IRS won't correct you if you don't use the most effective methods.

- *Charitable Giving* can be done in various ways, and some are clearly more prudent from a tax perspective. You don't need a massive family foundation to benefit from strategic charitable strategies.

These are the most critical facets of wealth planning. Every person, regardless of their net worth, needs to consider these key facets of their planning. Whether you use a Family Office or external advisors, these topics are crucial to address.

And Nothing You Don't

As you can see, we find significant overlap between the services provided by a Family Office for ultra-high-net-worth families and those needed by traditional high-net-worth clients. However, the delivery and execution of these services may look very different.

For instance, the ultra-high-net-worth client may have needs that don't make sense for traditional high-net-worth clients to pay for:

- Aviation Management
- Travel Management
- Property Management
- Chef and Meal Planning Services
- Bill Pay
- And more

While most or all of these sound exciting to include, very few clients who fit the more traditional definition of "wealthy" have need of or the desire to pay for them. They all come at a cost, often much higher than what a typical high-net-worth investor would be willing to pay. As such, The Efficient

Family Office doesn't worry about these types of services and recommends leaving them off your list as you structure your own financial team. So, let's explore more deeply the benefits and elements of The Efficient Family Office.

5

Maximizing Client Value: The Efficient Family Office Approach

arlier, we outlined the "Four Silent Killers," providing basic explanations of common challenges clients face when working with financial advisory teams. However, these examples barely scratch the surface of the issues we frequently encounter.

Imagine working with a financial advisor who manages your investments and touches lightly on other aspects of your financial life. They look into your estate planning, discuss tax strategies, and oversee your insurance needs. However, their involvement in these areas remains at a high level at best. Fortunately, the fee they charge seems fair.

But what if you discovered another firm that charges the exact same while offering more layers of service and value for your family? How would your financial situation transform if you felt like you had your own family office without actually hiring a vast team to work exclusively for you?

As we've discussed, these firms do exist, and they provide everything you need to avoid the Four Silent Killers. The benefits these firms can provide for high-net-worth families can not be overstated. Let's now look at the right way to integrate a next-level advisory team to manage your finances.

The Wealth Advisor Who Is a Wealth Advisor

While ultra-high-net-worth individuals seem to have the answer to the challenges clients face via a traditional Family Office, The Efficient Family Office offers the antidote to the Four Silent Killers. This means almost everyone in the high-net-worth category can have access to this higher level of wealth management. To illustrate the possibilities, let's contrast two scenarios a couple might face as they work with someone who calls himself or herself a wealth advisor.

Tom and Kate worked hard through their early years. They raised a great family and built a profitable business. When they reached their mid-50s, they had an opportunity to sell their company and realize so many of their dreams.

Their advisor, at the time, had served them since shortly after their marriage—a time when they were much younger and were just beginning to accumulate assets. Personable with an admirable reputation, the advisor had become a trusted friend over the years.

Tom and Kate's accountant had been with them almost as long. They trusted her to keep their books balanced, help them maneuver the tax laws, and give them accurate cash flow reports. They hadn't seen their estate attorney since their older child graduated from high school; however, he had checked every box at that time, so they were confident their affairs were in order.

They had added a second advisor when the business started to grow. The profitable years had allowed them to save a tidy sum, and they felt having two financial advisors, in addition to their accountant and attorney, meant they were getting the right advice from diverse perspectives.

However, as Tom and Kate began to more deeply explore selling their business, they started to see the disarray multiple voices can cause. Additionally, they began to face the problems of having an investment advisor with limited knowledge and resources. They needed someone who could handle the critical planning involved with their newly formed complexity. Without collaboration between the advisors and other professionals, Tom and Kate realized they'd missed some opportunities through the years.

A quick review revealed they hadn't updated the estate attorney about the current status of their growing family or the rapidly increasing value of their business. And those were only two key factors that contributed to planning opportunities. While their advisor had tremendous intentions, he didn't have a full knowledge of the importance of updating estate plans, and he never instigated meetings to review his clients' current financial situation or plans for the future. The financial advisor relationship was limited to reviews of portfolios and discussions about how the markets were doing. There were a few strategies they could have used, but in some cases, the window had closed on the opportunity.

Let's rewind Tom and Kate's story and take it through a different scenario—one in which they worked with a "wealth advisor who is actually a wealth advisor."

In this alternative timeline, Tom and Kate partnered with a firm that offered considerably more than traditional financial advice. Their primary advisor led a team of experts, fostering collaboration between their estate attorney, tax advisor, and the wealth management team. Utilizing The Efficient Family Office process, Tom and Kate engaged in standard planning activities alongside investment strategies, all while ensuring seamless collaboration among the professionals that handled their business affairs.

Tom and Kate capitalized on planning opportunities and leveraged their evolving business success to minimize tax implications and optimize their estate plan. Additionally, this comprehensive service didn't require more time or incur higher fees; many elite firms now offer such services as part of their standard fee structure.

Tom and Kate's story emphasizes the reality that what you don't feel can kill you. In the first scenario, they lived comfortably and felt successful as they watched their business grow. However, unbeknownst to them, they missed numerous opportunities by settling for the status quo. The saying "What you don't know can't hurt you" couldn't be more false when it comes to the state of your finances.

Finding an Advisor You Can't Outgrow

In the first scenario, Tom and Kate worked with a solo advisor who called himself a wealth manager. He truly did his best, and when Tom and Kate each had only simple 401(k)s and minimal liquid assets outside the business, their advisor provided adequate service. Regrettably, without the more elite financial team you find in The Efficient Family Office, when Tom and Kate grew the business, their planning needs became more than their well-intentioned advisor could handle.

The couple could have added a central firm that coordinated with their solo advisor to put themselves in a structure they couldn't outgrow. At the time, they didn't have a complex financial situation. They obviously didn't use all the services at their disposal, but they always had comfort knowing their advisor would be prepared if and when they did need them.

It didn't take long for Tom and Kate to use the firm's advanced planning opportunities and tax strategies. From the moment they had the idea for their business, their primary advisor consulted with the other professionals in his office to ensure Tom and Kate's grassroots business had the best chance of success.

As their net worth grew, they consulted with experts to prepare their business for sale, ensure assets were titled properly and structured in proper trusts, maximize the pre-tax opportunities inside of the business, and advance the level of investment strategy they considered as their liquid net worth increased. With The Efficient Family Office, Tom and Kate had confidence this advisory team would be in place for the duration of their wealth planning needs. There was no level of success or complexity this Efficient Family Office team was not prepared for.

With a primary advisor connecting with other experts in their respective fields, Tom and Kate's legacy grew tremendously more than it would have in the first scenario. At Kathmere, we recommend that any client considering a new advisor should plan for success well into the future and far beyond their current financial situation. Even if you are currently working with an advisor, it's vital to ensure a degree of durability exists in the relationship. It's much easier to change wealth managers early in the game than after you've outgrown your solo advisor.

Coordinated Planning Does Exist

The greatest benefit Tom and Kate received in the second scenario was the internal coordination and collaboration amongst investment, planning, operational, legal, and other advisors. In The Efficient Family Office, these experts all work in the same office for the same company and the same purpose. As discussed, while it may not be quite as deep as some facets of a true Family Office, this structure aims to replicate the critical components.

Many clients assume that if they have a financial advisor in one company, an estate attorney in another office, a tax advisor in a third, and an insurance broker and banker in two other locations, coordination simply isn't possible. This is categorically false. Coordination and information sharing are probably the most important facets of The Efficient Family Office. The key is to set it out as an intentional objective with a proven process that works.

At Kathmere, we bring these professionals together every day. On the investment side, our planning and investment team becomes listed as an interested party on any investment accounts not directly under our management. This is true whether the accounts are held with other advisors or are private investments made directly by the client, such as private equity, direct business investments, or real estate. By becoming an interested party, we have full access to statements, activity, tax information, and other relevant data. This allows us to make informed decisions about our client's broader picture. It also enables us to provide comprehensive reports regarding the household, proactive advice to the client, and information to other advisers when necessary.

Our advanced planning team works with new clients to gather all legal and estate planning documents. We immediately review and summarize these documents and create a client-friendly summary to use as a regular part of all our meetings. Our team takes time to become intimately aware of the client's personal life and aspirations as well as their financial life. This puts us in the best position to recognize impactful changes that might precipitate updates or changes to any legal documents or estate plans. Without this information, a breakdown can very easily happen.

Our planning team also immediately builds a relationship with the client's external CPAs and tax advisors. We keep an open line of communication with them so the full list of their client's accounts is on their radar. And because we've become interested parties on those accounts, we're able to provide information for both the accounts under our management and those managed by other firms. We provide summaries so they know when to expect various tax documents. And, thanks to technological advancements, we upload these documents to a secure portal so that other professionals can access them, and the client doesn't have to worry about this responsibility. Additionally, we prepare a year-end summary of potential or probable tax gains or loss harvesting opportunities. Then, we share the summary with the client's CPA to ensure any moves we make in investment accounts work with their broader tax strategy.

We also gather primary life and disability insurance documents for every new client. People often lose track of these critical aspects of wealth planning. We discuss the ownership of these policies as well as the beneficiary of the policies. We commonly see clients holding inefficient policies like term policies at or near the end of their useful life. Many clients also have permanent policies that aren't performing as originally intended because they have not been reviewed or checked for many years.

Most advisory firms, when asked, would assure you they could perform all these key coordinations. Sadly, too many would be figuring it out as they went because they've never offered such high-level, comprehensive service. However, without a built-in process and a team of experts, properly executing in so many areas is difficult at best.

The key to the success of this process is the advisory firm's experience—carrying out these steps on a regular basis for many clients. Modern technology has made our process significantly easier. And The Efficient Family Office believes this coordinated, comprehensive process is what clients need and deserve.

Taking Control of the Multitude of Voices

In Tom and Kate's first scenario, one of the primary hurdles they had to overcome was the silent killers of multiple advisors. The myth of employing a variety of professionals to be in a better financial position actually made it more difficult to reach the couple's dreams and ensure the maximization of their legacy. As we discussed, having multiple advisors actually puts tremendous pressure on the client because he or she is then required to coordinate the overall asset allocation. Like a man with five clocks attempting to figure out exactly what time it is, without training or a background in wealth management, the client is often forced to become the ultimate decision-maker.

In the second scenario, Tom and Kate found a primary advisor who handled everything holistically, coordinating the entire household. Even if Tom and Kate had kept all the advisors from the first scenario, a primary advisor with an awareness of every account, all their aspirations, and their constantly changing lifestyle would relieve them of the stress of dealing with potentially conflicting advice.

At Kathmere, we believe clients are better off with one central advisor, and we built our process to primarily act as the overall advisor. At the same time, we recognize situations will arise where it is not feasible or what the client is looking for. Some ultra-high-net-worth individuals respected their prior advisor relationship so much they didn't want to sever those ties. They knew they needed the additional value of the Kathmere process; however, they chose to retain additional advisors.

We thought it prudent to have a solution to meet the needs of these clients. To that end, The Efficient Family Office offers a solution many have opted to use. We suggest those who prefer more than one advisor use this structure in their financial team.

As previously mentioned, our first recommendation in taking control of the mess of multiple voices is setting up a Lead Advisor. We believe this role in the structure is of primary importance when working with multiple advisors at a variety of firms. Each advisor maintains autonomy to carry out their particular investment-related task; however, naming a lead advisor accomplishes critical key goals:

- One advisor sits in a position to know the full scope of all your accounts.
- All reports are based on the full family balance sheet.
- The client is relieved of the responsibility of determining household allocations.
- All key decisions and recommendations flow through a single advisor.
- Coordination of activities, including tax harvesting, is consolidated (as best possible) to ensure nothing is missed.

- All crucial financial pieces are represented in the estate planning process as the lead advisor works with the family's attorney.

So, what stops people from enlisting the services of a single lead advisor to streamline their financial picture and give them optimal service?

- Many clients don't know they can or should ask one of their advisors to take the lead.
- Some clients believe this kind of coordination will cost significantly more than they currently pay.
- Some existing advisors simply don't want the additional work and responsibility of becoming a lead advisor.
- Some advisors lack the expertise, capabilities, and depth of team necessary to carry out this demanding role.
- Some advisors work for a company that will not allow them to serve in this role.
- Advisors without a process in place to execute this challenging role may want to charge significantly more.

If you feel the pain of multiple voices in your financial planning, it's time to embrace the philosophy that one great advisor is better than two good ones, and if you choose to have more than one advisor, it is imperative to your financial health to select a Lead Advisor who has access to all your accounts, coordinates them to protect your future, and holds the reins of your finances. If you have multiple advisors and can't categorically state which one is in charge, it means none of them are. It's time to change this reality.

6

How to Build Your Own Efficient Family Office

Now that we've explored the unique challenges of managing a growing net worth and the implications of engaging an adequate advisor as opposed to a superb team of experts, let's look at the roles you will need in order to maximize your financial position. Firms like Kathmere Capital have spent years building and perfecting the process of The Efficient Family Office—a framework characterized by centralized strategy, collaboration, and a depth of team not often found. The wealth advisor assumes a central role, armed with insights into the client's values, family dynamics, and goals.

The experience of these elite firms and their dedication to bringing the best allow them to ensure their clients' plans are optimized to succeed and align with their future goals and legacy plans. Fortunately, Kathmere doesn't have a patent on the general concept of The Efficient Family Office. There are select other firms that are capable and have also chosen to serve their clients with this high-level style of management. Additionally, it's not impossible to replicate the process with your own people. You simply need to know what to do and the mechanics of how to make it work. But first, you'll need a few key components to make this a reality:

- Lead Wealth Advisor(s)
- Investment Specialist(s)
- Estate / Tax Specialist
- Operations Associate
- Reporting Tools
- A Proven Repeatable Process

Lead Advisor

A Lead Advisor may be the only person you work with; however, it could also be a primary person in charge of a multi-advisor team. Either way, this individual will be your overall coordinator. We recommend someone with a Certified Financial Planner (CFP) certification or an advisor with a very broad and holistic view of the wealth management landscape. Your first point of contact for all things financial, he or she will usually be involved in every decision and meeting regarding your accounts and, due to the work involved, will generally not serve in any other roles.

Investment Specialist

When looking for an investment specialist to work alongside your lead advisor, you'll want someone who has completed the post-graduate professional certification of Chartered Financial Analyst (CFA). This person will offer a high level of acumen on all financial topics. He or she will take charge of portfolios managed internally by the lead advisor as well as provide due diligence and oversight of more sophisticated external investments such as private equity, direct real estate investments, or other business investments. Within The Efficient Family Office process, investment specialists commonly review investment opportunities proposed to clients. At Kathmere, investment specialists provide this review even when the proposal has nothing to do with assets held and managed by our firm.

It is also important to note that on high-level teams, the Investment Specialist role does not work directly with their own clients. This person does not split their time working part of their day as Lead Wealth Advisor and part of their day as Investment Specialist. In the elite teams, Investment Specialists dedicate themselves fully to the key roles of investment strategy, ongoing diligence, and other key portfolio management responsibilities. We caution people to watch for two red flags when reviewing their wealth management team:

- *Beware of the person who serves many different roles.* As stated, the best teams have specialists handling different aspects of the job. Planning people focus on planning, investment specialists concentrate on investments, and estate/tax people remain in that realm. Too much crossover or claims that one person does it all can be a sign that the team lacks the depth to be able to do the job you may need.
- *Be cautious of "affiliated" team members.* This is a clever trick employed by many firms of all levels, particularly those affiliated with larger institutions. As an example, global institutions often post bios of investment and

research people in their New York office. While these specialists may share an employer with the person you will work with, usually, they share absolutely no relationship. They will never be involved in any aspects of the client's life or advice, and in many cases, the advisor you work with has never met or spoken to these people. It is truly a market spin used to increase the perception of the depth of the team. General research is a commodity now available to everyone and should not be confused with direct advice or high-level support.

In a process like The Efficient Family Office, you'll find more direct contact and in-office support for your team. These aspects allow you to more adequately judge the level of expertise that can truly serve your needs.

Estate / Tax Specialist

Many decisions you'll have to make regarding your financial future will have uncertain outcomes. In the world of investments, for example, even the most prudent of investments could go in the wrong direction for a period of time. In the same way, an utterly foolish investment can actually do well for a while. You won't really know the long-term results of your investments for many years down the road. In fact, when you enter most investments, the future outcome is completely unknown.

On the other side of the predictability spectrum are estate planning and tax strategy. When you complete an estate or tax planning strategy, the outcome is immediately known. It is quantitative and certain. As we stated before, because so many of the financial moves you make in your life are uncertain, nailing the palpable ones is a necessary step to a confident wealth plan.

A financial advisor properly armed with a knowledgeable team can proactively evaluate the needs of the client and then enlist the estate specialist to ensure that the client's plan for the future is a living, evolving document. With every dollar you accumulate and every family dynamic that changes, the strategy for your legacy has the potential to change.

Many clients may not immediately see the imperative nature of this specialist; however, no wealth planning team is truly adequate until it contains deep expertise in estate and tax planning. Unfortunately, some financial advisors tell clients they work closely with an attorney, and clients get trapped in the "good enough" approach. A financial advisor who works closely with an attorney will never rise to the level of having a legal expert on your advisory team who focuses solely on your future planning and doesn't charge an additional fee to do it.

Kathmere's Efficient Family Office includes a veteran estate and tax attorney with decades of experience in various private law firms. This obviously sophisticated level of expertise may not be easily replicated or available in the majority of advisory firms. However, with a bit of diligence, you can secure a team with this ultra-high level of specialist, and if you truly want to optimize your financial picture, this specialist must be on your list.

Operations

If you sense that your Lead Wealth Advisor, investment specialist, or any other key members of your advisory team also opens accounts, sends tax documents to your CPA, schedules meetings, sends wires, obtains statement copies, or assists in setting up your online login, immediately question the depth of their team. Key specialists do not have time to help fifty to one hundred clients take care of these administrative assistant-style tasks. The Efficient Family Office employs dedicated operation persons who work with clients on all non-advice-related needs. You want a team that gets involved in every aspect of your life that affects finances—so involved they focus one hundred percent of their time on strategy and advice. The operations specialists allow those valuable key players to avoid becoming burdened with administrative tasks.

Reporting Tools

The Efficient Family Office finds its identity in collaboration and coordination, and this is most effectively carried out in the ability to accurately report on the client's complete financial picture. Optimal reporting requires robust information gathering and organizing. The advanced technology available to financial advisors today must be utilized to ensure each member of the team can see how the various intricacies of the client's plan are working together. Powerful reporting tools make nearly every kind of report one can imagine. Let me share just a sampling of reports that Kathmere Capital builds and uses regularly as part of The Efficient Family Office process:

- Balance Sheet / Net Worth Report
- Goal and Cash Flow Status Reports
- Comprehensive Household Portfolio Reporting
- Private Investment Tracking: Committed and Called Capital
- Beneficiary Summary
- Life Insurance Tracker
- Estate Document Summary and Flowchart
- Investment Tax Tracking: Income (Dividends and Interest) and Capital Gains (Realized and Unrealized)

A Proven Repeatable Process

Not one part of anything I've shared in these pages has been registered for copyright or patent. Nor does it require proprietary knowledge or a product not available to the general public. Everything I've described is based purely on years of experience, development of expertise, and the ability to execute a service model that goes above and beyond. Still, my involvement in the industry has shown me how few have been able to consistently bring this kind of advanced team together and form a tested process using tools that allow them to deliver optimal comprehensive service to high net-worth clients.

Despite the inconsistency found in the industry, these elite firms ready to handle your specific financial needs do exist, and Kathmere Capital is just one. Using a series of questions and discussion points, you have the ability to find or build a structure that maximizes the value you receive from your financial advisory team.

In the next chapter, we will dive a bit deeper and give you the foundational inquiries you need to make to begin the exploration into finding your personal Efficient Family Office.

7

Don't Simply Ask Questions, Ask the Correct Questions

So far, I've uncovered the variety of pitfalls and fallaciously labeled minor inefficiencies in the financial industry and revealed the skeleton of The Efficient Family Office. Now, it's time for action. We never intended this book to merely disperse information. Instead, we want you to maximize the potential of your net worth starting today.

Though you don't yet feel the impact of financial inefficiencies, they loom large, waiting for you to discover their corrosive and deleterious impact. Unfortunately, without the proper tools, you may never fully see what you lost. The compounding effect of these small inefficiencies and missed opportunities should make someone with a higher degree of wealth shudder. But how do you know if your advisor is using the most innovative technology? Do they take advantage of software for the execution of mundane tasks, or do they still rely on their own ingenuity and time-consuming hours to get the job done? Worse still, are you paying for those hours of reporting that can be done digitally rather than putting those fees toward additional services?

We have developed questions for you to ask to avoid the Four Silent Killers of your financial status—from rating your current advisor to finding a Right Fit advisor and adding people to your team who can navigate estate planning and taxes. While you might not have the funds to set up a personal family office, by asking the correct questions, you can follow the bread trail of the ultra-rich and have your finances managed by an equally integrated and comprehensive team of experts.

Now that you understand the elements necessary to set up your own elite wealth management process, let's get started asking questions, gathering information, and arming ourselves with everything we need to know to make certain our wealth will serve us for our lifetime and leave a powerful legacy after we're gone.

What Will Your Advisor and His Team Do for You?

As we mentioned, it's essential to differentiate between advisors who offer comprehensive planning and those who provide narrow, simplistic services. Understanding the scope of your advisor's services is critical. Does your advisor offer holistic financial planning, including investment management, estate planning, tax strategy, and insurance oversight? Or do they focus solely on a specific area, such as investment management?

The biggest challenge is that most don't put out big flashing lights listing their limitations. No one adds "things we're not strong in" next to their strengths on their website or business card. Instead, you get generic titles such as financial, wealth, or investment advisor, and you're left to figure out their level of ability on your own. By asking a few questions, you can make a more informed decision:

Typical Clients

- Are you able to serve as a Lead Advisor if that structure is of interest?
- Do you do that for other clients?
- Can you demonstrate to me how you do that, or can you introduce me to one of those clients?

The Advisory Team

- Do you have a team, and if so, who will work with me personally and be my primary contact?
- How many individuals will be taking care of my specific situation?
  - This helps to ensure continuity. A small team, where only one person knows about you, is usually not ideal.
- Are each of these individuals truly part of your in-house team, or are you telling me about someone in a remote office who will never deal directly with my situation?
  - This tactic is particularly common at larger companies as a marketing technique. They will list research, investment, or strategy people who do not work at all with the advisor and will never be involved in your situation.

- Is each person on the team in the same office, or are they dispersed across locations?
- What does each person on the advisor's team do?
  - For each professional, ask about their expertise and experience in the specific area they cover, including planning, investments, tax, estate, and so on.
  - If one person covers too many roles, consider that a red flag.
- How will I interact with each member of the team? Will they be available for meetings or calls when needed?
- What credentials do the members of your team hold? CFP®, CPWA, CFA, JD, LLM, and more? (These are the most respected designations; you may want to question others not on this list.)
- What is their background and experience?
  - This question helps ensure they have been in this industry for a while and haven't been hopping from one financial endeavor to another.

Collaboration with Other Advisors

- How will you interact and collaborate with my other advisors—internally and externally?
  - CPA / Tax Advisors
  - Estate Advisors
  - Insurance Brokers
  - Bankers (if applicable)
- What level of estate or tax planning strategy is your team able to perform? Who does this, and what are their qualifications/experience?
- Can you show me an example of a review of a legal document or estate planning summary?

How Will This Team Optimize Your Wealth?

Once we understand what the advisor we interview will do for us, we need to find out how they plan to serve. These questions encompass their investment process, financial planning approach, and the overall methodology behind their advisory services.

Investment Strategy

- What process do you use to invest my money?
- What is your investment philosophy?
- What strategies do you employ to manage risk and pursue returns? How do you conduct financial planning?
- When and how often do you believe we should meet?
  - Does that differ by topic? Investment vs. tax vs. estate?
- Do you report on assets and holdings not held with your firm? If so, how is this done?
- Does your company allow you to review investments you aren't managing?
- What level of investment diligence can you help me with if I have opportunities to invest outside of what you offer?
- Can you provide an example of some diligence you have performed in the past?
- Can and will you become an "Interested Party" on accounts not managed by your firm?

Reporting Tools and Process

- What tools and techniques will you use to assess my financial situation and develop a personalized plan?

- What investment reports do you provide on a regular basis that are above and beyond the normal statements I receive for my accounts?
  - Can these reports be customized to my needs?
  - Can I see a sample?
  - Do the reports reflect assets not managed by the advisor?
- Can you show me a sample of some of the non-investment reporting?
  - Balance sheet / net worth
  - Estate plan summary / Flowchart
  - Insurance summary
  - Private Investment Tracker / Capital Call Summary

Understanding Your Advisor's Business Model

In the world of financial advice, understanding your advisor's business model is crucial to making informed decisions about your financial future. While the questions above lay the groundwork, it's important to dig deeper.

Because the financial advisory landscape is diverse, advisors operate under various business models. Some work for large multinational institutions, such as global banks, while others are part of smaller boutique organizations. Differences in offerings, conflicts of interest, fee levels, and overall approach can vary significantly from one firm to another. As a client, it's crucial to understand these distinctions and consider them carefully before making decisions.

The key lies in asking the right questions to gain clarity so you can make informed choices that align with your goals and values.

Understanding the Advisor Business Model

- Is the advisor independent or affiliated with a large global bank? Is the advisor or firm affiliated with a company that manages and focuses on proprietary investments? Is the advisor independent?
- What does the advisor consider to be the main advantages of the business model and affiliations they currently operate under?
- What would the advisor consider the main downsides to the model and affiliations?
- Has the advisor you are interviewing worked under the same business model for his or her entire career? Why or why not?
- Has the advisor worked with the same firm for his or her entire career? Why or why not?
- Does the business model impact recommendations the advisor makes?
  - Does the firm employ any of its own strategies?
  - If so, how do you measure them, and how do you decide to exit funds managed by your own firm?
- How do the advisor and the firm get paid for their services?

You have always been in control of your financial future; however, I hope I have raised your awareness of the fact, and you are now more prepared to ask the right questions and create a more accurate vision for what's possible in your financial life. I want you to be in the best position possible to understand the industry and take an educated and solid next step. It's time to ask yourself, "How can I find a team that practices the philosophy of the Family Office structure without building it on my own?" and "How would my future change if I worked with a firm structured to maximize the value provided to clients?"

8

You Deserve More

It's time.

Time to expect more.

Time to experience more.

If you take only one thing from this book, I hope it's the message that you deserve more. You should demand and expect excellence from the professionals you pay to manage your wealth. More than anything, I don't want to see anyone settle for the status quo. It's time to set higher, loftier goals and know that they are attainable with the right team in place. Today is the day to optimize your financial advisory team and experience the excellence you deserve.

Not long ago, advisors worked for companies that are household names. They commonly had a one or two-person team with an administrative person supporting them. That outdated model still employs some competent, proficient, and highly intelligent people. Sadly, I believe the clients they work with receive less. They miss out on the optimization available in the modern financial advisory world.

I implore you to take what you've read to heart and compare it to the structure of your current financial advisory relationships. Use the questions and descriptions we've given to help you discern the difference between average, adequate, and advanced.

If you have experienced financial success through years of saving or accumulating wealth in other ways, you should not settle for average or even adequate. You deserve an advanced advisory team that offers excellence. The stakes are high, and incremental improvements truly multiply over time.

Working with Kathmere Capital

At Kathmere Capital, we use The Efficient Family Office process to squeeze out every last bit for our clients. We want perfect estate plans and optimal tax strategies. And we believe our client's investments should perform at the maximum level based on their desired level of risk. As we've mentioned, Kathmere Capital's simple yet powerful motto, "Everything you need, nothing you don't," encapsulates our approach to delivering tailored financial advice and solutions. Firms like ours provide every service and role we mentioned in chapter six by employing a team of experts in each of the key areas.

The Efficient Family Office focuses on providing essential services that truly add value to our clients' lives. In essence, The Efficient Family Office model at Kathmere Capital Management represents a paradigm shift in wealth management. By offering everything our clients need and nothing they don't, we empower them to navigate the complexities of their financial lives with confidence and clarity. With our team of experts by their side, our clients can rest assured that their financial future is in capable hands.

For many, reflecting on their current advisory team and comparing it to a team like ours, which includes multiple investment specialists, advanced planners, an estate attorney, and operations and money movement specialists, makes the decision clear. The value proposition becomes evident. Who doesn't want to pay the same fee for more services that provide comprehensive management for every aspect of your financial life?

Kathmere Capital would certainly welcome the opportunity to discuss your financial future. If not, we hope this book helps you find exactly what you need to avoid compounding inefficiencies and make the most of an expert wealth management team.

Take Control of Your Finances

You have always been in control of your financial future; however, my hope, as I write, is that you are now more aware of the possibilities and are also prepared to ask the right questions and create a more accurate vision for what's possible in your financial life. I want you to be in the best position available to understand the industry and take an educated and solid next step. More than anything, I don't want to see anyone settle for the status quo. It's time to set higher, loftier goals and know they are attainable with the right team in place.

You deserve a team that supports your lofty dreams of giving a monumental gift to charity or funding the education for an entire generation of your family. Regardless of your aspirations, do not settle for an advisory relationship that forces you to settle for less than the best.

As you embark on this journey, I hope you'll be motivated to diligently search for a team that takes advantage of every technological advancement and collaboration opportunity to serve you better. Remember, too, that a full-service firm doesn't necessarily equal higher cost. In our experience, it's the truly client-centered companies that also find a way to price their services in a manner that allows them to do more for less.

The Efficient Family Office champions a holistic approach to wealth management—one that transcends the narrow confines of specialized expertise. We advocate for a comprehensive strategy that addresses every facet of your financial life, from investments to estate planning and everything in between.

So, I pose a question to you: Why settle for less? Why not entrust your wealth to a firm that is constantly striving to advance and improve? As you turn the final page of this book, I want more for you than to simply appreciate Kathmere as a firm. I hope you feel inspired by the journey we've embarked upon together as you've read. Kathmere is more than simply a financial services provider. We're a partner in our clients' success, committed to guiding them—and you—through every stage of their financial journey. And for my team at Kathmere Capital and what we have built in The Efficient Family Office, I am immensely proud and grateful.

About the Author

Michael McDermott has been in the wealth management industry for 25 years and serves as the Chief Executive Officer of Kathmere Capital Management. In this role, he leads the strategic vision of Kathmere and works directly with many of the firm's important client relationships. Additionally, he sits on the firm's Investment Committee and Compliance Committee.

Michael graduated from St. Joseph's University as a member of the golf team, where he was named an All-American Scholar in his senior year. He was inducted into the University Athletics Hall of Fame. Michael is active in the community as a board member of The Cobbs Creek Restoration Foundation as well as a co-founder of The Golf Bridge Society. He remains an active and competitive golfer and can also be found coaching youth basketball in the winter months. Michael lives in Wayne, PA, with his wife and three sons.

WANT TO LEARN MORE ABOUT
THE EFFICIENT FAMILY OFFICE?

Visit kathmere.com
OR
call us at 610-989-3900

THIS BOOK IS PROTECTED INTELLECTUAL PROPERTY

The author of this book values Intellectual Property. The book you just read is protected by Instant IP™, a proprietary process, which integrates blockchain technology giving Intellectual Property "Global Protection." By creating a "Time-Stamped" smart contract that can never be tampered with or changed, we establish "First Use" that tracks back to the author.

Instant IP™ functions much like a Pre-Patent™ since it provides an immutable "First Use" of the Intellectual Property. This is achieved through our proprietary process of leveraging blockchain technology and smart contracts. As a result, proving "First Use" is simple through a global and verifiable smart contract. By protecting intellectual property with blockchain technology and smart contracts, we establish a "First to File" event.

Protected by Instant IP™

LEARN MORE AT INSTANTIP.TODAY

Made in the USA
Las Vegas, NV
12 January 2025

16284903R00050